Descendants of William Newton Edwards

Generation 1

1. **WILLIAM NEWTON**[1] **EDWARDS** was born about 1773 in Orange County, North Carolina. He died in 1855 in Russell County, Alabama. He married Mary Whatley, daughter of Michael Whatley and Hannah Rhodes in 1798 in Talbot County, Georgia. She was born about 1776 in Orange County, North Carolina. She died in 1850 in Dale County, Alabama.

More About William Newton Edwards:
Living In: 1830 Talbot County, Georgia
Living In: 1840 Talbot County, Georgia
Living In: 1850 Living with his son, Wilson B. Edwards, in Russell County, Alabama
Military Service: Second Regiment, Beaufort County, North Carolina Militia, War of 1812

Notes for William Newton Edwards:
Living with his son, Wilson B. Edwards, in the 1850 Russell County, Alabama, U.S. census with age listed as 77 years old and birth place as North Carolina.

William Newton Edwards and Mary Whatley had the following children:

2.   i. JAMES YOUNG[2] EDWARDS was born on 20 Aug 1799 in Wilkes County, Georgia. He died on 13 Jun 1879 in Lee County, Alabama. He married (1) MARY PERDUE on 20 Jun 1822 in Jones County, Georgia. She was born on 08 Nov 1801 in Georgia. She died on 21 May 1865 in Lee County, Alabama. He married (2) ELIZA DUNLAP on 31 Aug 1865 in Russell County, Alabama. She was born in 1814 in South Carolina. She died on 26 Dec 1873 in Lee County, Alabama. He married (3) LAUTICIA TAYLOR, daughter of Thomas Taylor on 29 Oct 1876 in Lee County, Alabama. She was born about 1845 in Georgia.

3.   ii. NANCY EDWARDS was born on 12 Aug 1801 in Georgia. She died about 1883 in Texas. She married Phillip M. Long on 20 Jun 1819 in Jones County, Georgia.

4.   iii. JOHN EDWARDS was born on 04 Mar 1803 in Georgia. He died in 1857 in Talbot County, Georgia. He married MARY OLIVER. She was born about 1808 in Georgia. She died in 1872 in Talbot County, Georgia.

5.   iv. AMBROSE EDWARDS was born on 16 Apr 1805 in Wilkes County, Georgia. He died on 06 Oct 1884 in Dale County, Alabama. He married Emeline James Gaulding, daughter of John Gaulding and Martha Gaulding in 1827 in South Carolina. She was born on 10 Feb 1810 in Virginia. She died on 01 Jan 1886 in Dale County, Alabama.

    v. WILLIAM EDWARDS was born on 28 Jan 1807 in Georgia.

6.   vi. MICHAEL EDWARDS was born on 24 Mar 1810 in Georgia. He died in 1854 in Russell County, Alabama. He married Matilda Adams on 01 Oct 1837 in Talbot County, Georgia. She was born on 20 Dec 1821 in North Carolina. She died on 03 Mar 1901 in Alabama.

    vii. JEMIMA EDWARDS was born in Jan 1813 in Georgia. She died in Alabama. She married Ezekiel Brown on 21 Aug 1831 in Talbot County, Georgia.

7.   viii. MARY EDWARDS was born on 16 May 1815 in Georgia. She died before 18 Feb 1875 in Alabama. She married WILLIAM ROBINSON. He was born about 1815. He died before 25 Jan 1850. She married (2) WILLIAM C. CLEGHORN on 08 Sep 1852 in

Russell County, Alabama. He was born on 22 Apr 1832 in Hall County, Georgia. He died on 19 Jul 1910 in Macon County, Alabama.

8. ix. ELIZABETH EDWARDS was born about 1818 in Georgia. She died after 03 Jun 1880. She married (1) WILLIAM TROTTER, son of William Trotter and (unknown) on 28 Dec 1843 in Talbot County, Georgia. He died in 1848. She married (2) FELSTON PARKER on 19 Dec 1849 in Russell County, Alabama. He was born on 12 Dec 1815 in North Carolina. He died before 09 Aug 1870.

9. x. SPENCER EDWARDS was born on 03 Apr 1817 in Georgia. He died on 02 Nov 1897 in Taylor County, Georgia. He married Mary Ann Willis, daughter of John E. Willis and Susanna H. Biggs on 25 Apr 1836 in Talbot County, Georgia. She was born about 1821 in Georgia. She died before 1880.

10. xi. WILSON B. EDWARDS was born on 27 Jun 1821 in Georgia. He died on 16 Sep 1863 in Russell County, Alabama. He married Eleanor Aurora Trotter, daughter of William Trotter and (unknown) on 10 Aug 1843. She was born on 11 Apr 1823 in Russell County, Alabama. She died on 27 Oct 1873.

Generation 2

2. **JAMES YOUNG**[2] **EDWARDS** (William Newton[1]) was born on 20 Aug 1799 in Wilkes County, Georgia. He died on 13 Jun 1879 in Lee County, Alabama. He married (1) **MARY PERDUE** on 20 Jun 1822 in Jones County, Georgia. She was born on 08 Nov 1801 in Georgia. She died on 21 May 1865 in Lee County, Alabama. He married (2) **ELIZA DUNLAP** on 31 Aug 1865 in Russell County, Alabama. She was born in 1814 in South Carolina. She died on 26 Dec 1873 in Lee County, Alabama. He married (3) **LAUTICIA TAYLOR**, daughter of Thomas Taylor on 29 Oct 1876 in Lee County, Alabama. She was born about 1845 in Georgia.

More About James Young Edwards:
Cause Of Death: ; Pneumonia
Living In: 1830 Talbot County, Georgia
Living In: 1840 Talbot County, Georgia
Living In: 1866 Russell County, Alabama
Occupation: 1850 in Russell County, Alabama; Farmer
Occupation: 1860 in Russell County, Alabama; Farmer
Occupation: 1870 in Salem, Lee County, Alabama; Farmer
Property: 1850 in Russell County, Alabama; 100 Acres Improved and 60 Acres Unimproved
Property: 1860 in Russell County, Alabama; 200 Acres Improved and 80 Acres Unimproved
Property: 1880 in Lee County, Alabama; 100 Acres Improved and 60 Acres Unimproved

Notes for James Young Edwards:
Moved from Talbot County Georgia to Russell County, Alabama in 1844. This part of Russell County is now in Lee County, Alabama.

There is a June 1880 Productions of Agriculture report that shows Young Edwards having 100 Acres Improved and 60 Acres Unimproved in Lee County, Alabama. Possibly this is his estate.

1880 property record is from 1880 Lee County Productions of Agriculture that was posted after his death.

Lived in Bibb County, Georgia after his first marriage and moved to Talbot County, Georgia in 1827. Moved to Russell County, Alabama in 1844.

Notes for Mary Perdue:
Rev. Cherry in "The History of Opelika" gives Mary's date of death as May 21, 1865.

Rev. Cherry in "The History of Opelika" gives her last name as Perdien but marriage record has Purdue.

More About James Young Edwards and Mary Perdue:
Marriage License: 20 Jun 1822 in Jones County, Georgia
Marriage Fact: Married by D. T. Milling, J.P.

James Young Edwards and Mary Perdue had the following children:

    i. GREEN B.[3] EDWARDS was born on 04 May 1823 in Georgia. He died on 15 Feb 1885 in Lee County, Alabama. He married Mary Maude Wilson, daughter of James Wilson and (unknown) on 01 Oct 1846 in Russell County, Alabama. She was born on 13 Jun 1832 in Georgia. She died on 27 Oct 1896 in Baird, Callahan County,Texas.

    More About Green B. Edwards:
    Burial: Salem Cemetery, Salem, Lee County, Alabama
    Occupation: 1850 in Russell County, Alabama; Farmer
    Occupation: 1860 in Russell County, Alabama; Farmer
    Occupation: 1870 in Salem, Lee County, Alabama; Farmer
    Occupation:1880 in Meadows Cross Roads, Lee County, Alabama; Farmer
    Property: 1850 in Russell County, Alabama; 40 Acres Improved and 80 Acres Unimproved

    ii. MISSOURI (MASOURA) ELIZABETH EDWARDS was born on 24 Oct 1824 in Georgia. She died on 09 Apr 1873 in Alabama. She married Richard E. Hightower, son of Raleigh Hightower and Martha Frances Robinson on 16 Nov 1852 in Russell County, Alabama. He was born on 29 Jul 1832 in Georgia. He died on 25 Feb 1910 in Crenshaw County, Alabama.

    Notes for Missouri (Masoura) Elizabeth Edwards:
    Headstone reads - IN MEMORY OF - MASOURA - WIFE OF - RICHARD HIGHTOWER.

    1850 U.S. census lists her name as Masouri.

    DEATH AND OBITUARY NOTICES FROM THE SOUTHERN CHRISTIAN ADVOCATE 1867-1878 Issue of May 28, 1873

    Missouri Elizabeth Hightower, daughter of Young and Mary Edwards, of Lee County, Ala., was born October 23d, 1824 married to Richard Hightower in 1853, died April 9, 1873. She leaves an aged father, husband and three children.

    Headstone has birthdate of February 4, 1823. Obituary has birthdate of October 24, 1824. February 4, 1823 would conflict with birthdate of her brother Green B. Edwards.

    ----

    iii. WILLIAM HENRY C. EDWARDS was born on 02 Nov 1826 in Georgia. He died on 01 Nov 1898. He married Caroline M. Roper, daughter of John Thompson Roper and Elizabeth C. Estes on 15 Dec 1848 in Macon County, Alabama. She was born on

21 Mar 1832 in Alabama. She died on 10 Nov 1892.

More About William Henry C. Edwards:
Burial: 02 Nov 1898 in Pine Grove Cemetery, Phenix City,
Alabama
Occupation: 1860 in Russell County, Alabama; Farmer
Occupation: 1870 in Salem, Lee County, Alabama; Farmer
Occupation: 1880 in Salem, Lee County, Alabama; Farmer

iv.　JOHN WESLEY EDWARDS was born on 01 Jan 1829 in Georgia. He died in 1863 in Montgomery, Alabama. He married Mary Ann Watson on 21 Sep 1848.

More About John Wesley Edwards:
Occupation:1860; Farmer, Russell County, Alabama
Military Service: Soldier C.S.A.

Notes for John Wesley Edwards:
Confederate Soldier- died in hospital in Montgomery, Alabama.

v.　GEORGIA A.V. EDWARDS was born on 25 Jun 1832 in Georgia. She died on 25 Aug 1847 in Lee County, Alabama.

vi.　GEORGE W . EDWARDS was born on 17 Jul 1834 in Georgia. He died on 26 Nov 1904 in Macon County, Alabama. He married (1) CORDELIA HUDSON on 03 Oct 1861. She was born on 18 Aug 1844 in Salem, Alabama. She died on 27 Mar 1924 in Macon County, Georgia. He married (2) JULIA A. COOPER on 16 Oct 1856 in Macon County, Georgia. She was born on 08 Jan 1834. She died on 25 Jun 1860.

More About George W . Edwards:
Burial: Society Hill Baptist Cemetery, Society Hill, Macon County,
Alabama
Occupation: 1880 in Salem, Lee County, Alabama; Farmer
Occupation:1900 in Loachapoka, Lee County, Alabama; Census
Enumerator
Military Service: Company K, 34th Alabama Infantry, C.S.A.

Notes for George W . Edwards:
George is the enumerator listed on the 1900 U.S. census sheet that includes his family.

vii.　RALEIGH H. EDWARDS was born on 17 Jul 1837 in Georgia. He died on 19 May 1862 in Richmond, Virginia.

More About Raleigh H. Edwards:
Military Service: Company C, 6th Alabama Infantry, C.S.A.

Notes for Raleigh H. Edwards:
Died May 19, 1862 in Richmond, Virginia. Buried by brother, Robert L. Edwards, who was also serving in Company C, 6th Alabama Infantry.

viii.　ROBERT L. EDWARDS was born on 04 Jul 1839 in Georgia. He died on 31 May 1862 in Virginia.

More About Robert L. Edwards:
Military Service: Company C, 6th Alabama Infantry, C.S.A.

Notes for Robert L. Edwards:
Killed during the Battle of Seven Pines.
Sergeant when he was killed on May 31, 1862

    ix.   MARY JANE EDWARDS was born on 09 Nov 1844 in Alabama. She died on 17 Oct 1868.

        Notes for Mary Jane Edwards:
        Never Married.

More About James Young Edwards and Eliza Dunlap:
Marriage License: 28 Aug 1865 in Russell County, Alabama
Marriage Fact: Married by M. Y. Britt, M.G.

More About Lauticia Taylor:
Living In: 1880 Salem, Lee County, Alabama

Notes for Lauticia Taylor:
Rev. Cherry in "The History Of Opelika" gives marriage date as October 20, 1876.

Spelling of her first name is from her signature on her husband's probate records.

More About James Young Edwards and Lauticia Taylor:
Marriage Fact: Marriage performed by J. H. Lockhart

3.   NANCY[2] EDWARDS (William Newton[1]) was born on 12 Aug 1801 in Georgia. She died about 1883 in Texas. She married Phillip M. Long on 20 Jun 1819 in Jones County, Georgia.

More About Nancy Edwards:
Living In: 04 Jun 1880 With her grandson, J.A. Crouch, and his family in Harrison County, Texas.

More About Phillip M. Long:
Living In: 1830 Talbot County, Georgia

More About Phillip M. Long and Nancy Edwards:
Marriage License: 18 Jun 1819 in Jones County,
Georgia Marriage Fact: Married by H. Candler, J.P.

Phillip M. Long and Nancy Edwards had the following child:
    i.   NANCY[3] LONG. She married (UNKNOWN) CLEGG.

4.   JOHN[2] EDWARDS (William Newton[1]) was born on 04 Mar 1803 in Georgia. He died in 1857 in Talbot County, Georgia. He married **MARY OLIVER**. She was born about 1808 in Georgia. She died in 1872 in Talbot County, Georgia.

More About John Edwards:
Burial: Edwards Cemetery, Talbotton, Georgia
Living In: 1830 Talbot County, Georgia
Living In: 1840 Talbot County, Georgia
Occupation: 1850 in Talbot County, Georgia; Farmer

More About Mary Oliver:
Burial: Edwards Cemetery, Talbotton, Georgia
Occupation: 1860 in Talbotton, Talbot County, Georgia; Farmer
Occupation: 1870 in Talbotton, Talbot County, Georgia; Farmer
Property: 1860 in District 685, Talbot County, Georgia; 300 Acres Improved and 90
Acres Unimproved
Property: 1870 in Talbot County, Georgia; 300 Acres Improved and 100 Acres Unimproved

John Edwards and Mary Oliver had the following children:

    i.   AMANDA MELVINA[3] EDWARDS was born on 07 Sep 1824. She died on 25 Aug 1902 in Jackson Parish, Louisiana. She married Christopher Columbus Chambless, son of Jeptha Columbus Chambless and Susannah Jones on 16 Nov 1841 in Muskogee County, Georgia. He was born on 11 Jan 1820 in Warren County, Georgia. He died on 04 Mar 1909 in Jackson Parish, Louisiana.

        More About Amanda Melvina Edwards:
        Burial: Chambless Cemetery - near Eros, Jackson Parish, Louisiana

    ii.   AMBROSE JAMES EDWARDS was born on 29 Dec 1825 in Georgia. He married Arte Ann Chambless, daughter of Jeptha Columbus Chambless and Susannah Jones on 19 Oct 1843 in Talbot County, Georgia. She was born on 24 May 1828 in Warren County, Georgia.

        More About Ambrose James
        Edwards: b: 1826
        Occupation: 1850 in Talbot County, Georgia; Farmer
        Occupation: 1860 in Schley County, Georgia; Farmer
        Occupation: 1870 in Schley County, Georgia; Farmer
        Occupation: 1880 in Coldwater, Chattooga County, Georgia; Farmer
        Military Service: Bet. 04 Mar 1862-01 May 1865; Company B, 46th
        Georgia Infantry, C.S.A.

        Notes for Ambrose James Edwards:

        Mustered out of 46th Georgia Infantry May 1, 1865 at Greensboro, North Carolina.

    iii.   SARAH ANN EDWARDS was born on 27 Dec 1827 in Talbot County, Georgia. She died on 07 Mar 1859 in Louvale, Stewart County, Georgia. She married Jeptha Columbus Chambless, son of Jeptha Columbus Chambless and Susannah Jones on 19 Sep 1844 in Talbot County, Georgia. He was born on 08 Jul 1823 in Warren County, Georgia. He died on 23 Feb 1877 in Stewart County, Georgia.

    iv.   YOUNG NEWTON EDWARDS was born in 1830 in Talbot County, Georgia. He died before 11 Jun 1900. He married CLARKEY ANN ELIZABETH MOBLEY. She was born on 29 Sep 1842 in Georgia. She died on 17 Feb 1868. He married (2) SARAH VIRGINIA CLEGG, daughter of Anthony Clegg and Caroline Chaderton on 06 Feb 1872 in

Muscogee County, Georgia. She was born on 18 Mar 1851 in Harpers
Ferry, Virginia. She died on 09 Mar 1928 in Waco, Texas.

More About Young Newton Edwards:
Occupation: 1860 in Talbotton, Talbot County, Georgia; Farmer
Occupation: 1870 in Valley District, Talbot County, Georgia;
Farmer
Occupation: 1880 in Talbot County, Georgia; Farmer
Military Service: Bet. 04 May 1862-01 May 1865 ; Company I, 46th
Georgia Infantry, C.S.A.
Property: 1860 in District 685, Talbot County, Georgia; 80 Acres Improved and
250 Acres Unimproved
Property: 1880 in District 889, Talbot County, Georgia; 50 Acres Improved and
170 Acres Unimproved

Notes for Young Newton Edwards:
Enlisted in Company I. 46th Georgia Infantry at Talbotton, Talbot County,
Georgia May 4, 1862 and paroled May 1, 1865 at Greensboro, North Carolina.

v.   MARY ANN EDWARDS was born on 28 Sep 1832 in Georgia. She died on 22 Jan
      1910. She married Charles Tallie Cotten, son of George Cotten and Susannah
      Gibson on 17 Mar 1852 in Upson County, Georgia. He was born on 22 Apr 1826
      in Georgia. He died on 31 May 1870 in Ozark, Alabama.

      More About Mary Ann Edwards:
      Burial: Ozark, Alabama
      Living In:1880 With her children in Westville, Dale County, Alabama
      Living In: 1900 Westville, Dale County, Alabama

      Notes for Mary Ann Edwards:
      1900 U.S. census has April 1832 for month and year of birth.

vi.   JOHN W. EDWARDS was born on 18 Feb 1838.

      More About John W. Edwards:
      Living In: 1860 Living next door to his mother with Simon Castleberry and his
      family in Talbot County, Georgia
      Occupation: Farmer
      Military Service: March 4, 1862 until July 19, 1862 Company I, 46th Georgia
      Infantry, C.S.A.

      Notes for John W. Edwards:
      Discharged from Company I, 46th Georgia Infantry on July 19, 1862 due to
      poor eyesight and poor hearing.

      Enlisted at Talbotton, Talbot County, Georgia.

vii. HENRY HARRISON EDWARDS was born on 27 Jun 1840 in Talbot County, Georgia. He
      married Elizabeth Boswell on 09 Jul 1871 in Talbot County, Georgia. She was
      born in Nov 1848 in Talbot County, Georgia. She died in Talbot County, Georgia.

More About Henry Harrison Edwards:
Occupation: 1880 in Talbotton, Talbot County, Georgia; Farmer

viii.   WILLIAM SANFORD EDWARDS was born on 13 Jun 1843 in Talbot County, Georgia. He died on 08 Apr 1919 in Georgia. He married Harriett M. (unknown) about 1872. She was born on 07 Feb 1850 in Georgia. She died on 13 Mar 1908 in Georgia.

More About William Sanford Edwards:
Burial: Mount Vernon Cemetery, Schley County, Georgia
Occupation: 1870 in Talbotton, Talbot County, Georgia; Working on his mother's farm
Occupation: 1880 in Macon County, Georgia; Farmer
Occupation: 1900 in Macon County, Georgia; Farmer
Occupation: 1910 in Ideal, Macon County, Georgia; Farmer
Military Service: March 4, 1862 until April 26, 1865, Company I, 46th Georgia Infantry, C.S.A.

Notes for William Sanford Edwards:
Twin Brother of Milton Edwards.

ix.   MILTON BROWN EDWARDS was born on 13 Jun 1843 in Talbot County, Georgia. He died on 09 Mar 1911 in Talbotton, Georgia. He married Anne Eliza Hall on 19 Mar 1878 in Talbot County, Georgia. She was born on 07 Feb 1855 in Georgia. She died on 11 Mar 1929 in Georgia.

More About Milton Brown Edwards:
Burial: 10 Mar 1911 in Talbotton City Cemetery, Talbotton, Talbot County, Georgia
Occupation: 1870 in Talbotton, Talbot County, Georgia; Working on his mother's farm
Occupation: 1880 in Talbotton, Talbot County, Georgia; Farmer
Occupation: 1900 in Talbotton, Talbot County, Georgia; Farmer
Occupation: 1910 in Talbot County, Georgia; Retired
Military Service: Bet. 04 Mar 1862-26 Apr 1865 ; Company I, 46th Georgia Infantry, C.S.A.

Notes for Milton Brown Edwards:
Twin Brother of William Edwards.

The Talbotton New Era
Thursday,   March   16,
1911 Page One

Milton Brown Edwards

When the writer first came to Talbotton he used to talk every day with a man whom everybody called "Uncle Mit Edwards." He was an interesting talker, and had many things to tell of the old times of our fathers and mothers.

He had passed up along the pathway of life from the morning when the dewdrops of hope glisten like diamonds in the sun, along the past the noonday milestone where man is striving with all his might and main to win the prizes of life before the sunset of death ends his journey. He had passed all these stages along the way and had started down the gentle incline toward the grave, where all the shadows point backward when I first knew him. As the shadows in the life of an older person point backward, so does the memory and becoming childlike again in their simplicity and sincerity all their conversations are reminiscent with the things of long ago.

That's why I loved to talk with "Uncle Mit." He was interesting to me because I learned something by talking with him.

But his kind are passing fast away. Those who fought the battles of the sixties are growing fewer every day. Soon the fast re-echoing footstep will be heard as it passes over the dividing line between life and eternity. Most of the persons known to these grand old patriots have already preceded them. It was true of "Uncle Mit's" friends.

Mr. Edwards was born in Talbot county on the 13th day of June, 1843. He served in the Civil War. He was married to Miss Anne Eliza Hall, and to this union was born the following children: Mrs. Isabel Allen, Edgar H., Mary Lilyan, Clarence Brown and Oscar Davis Edwards. These with Mrs. Edwards, still survives him. He has also a living twin brother, Mr. William Edwards of Marion County and Mr. Taylor Edwards of San Antonio, Texas.

Mr. Edwards had been in failing health for four years. His condition did not become serious until a few days ago.

He passed peacefully into the regions of death at his home in the western part of town on the evening of March 9.

He was laid to rest in Oak Hill cemetery Friday afternoon at four o'clock. Rev. Graham Forrester conducted the funeral exercises.

The Talbotton New Era
Thursday, March 16, 1911
Page Three

Card of Thanks

We wish to express our heartfelt thanks to our loving friends and neighbors, who so kindly assisted us during the recent sickness and death of our beloved husband and father.

Mrs. M.B. Edwards and Family

----

x. LAFAYETTE TAYLOR EDWARDS was born on 14 Jul 1849 in Talbot County, Georgia. He died on 24 Jul 1916 in San Antonio, Texas. He married Frances Augusta Lightner, daughter of Thomas Sumpter Lightner and Nancy Bishop on 24 Dec 1869 in Barbour County, Alabama. She was born on 06 Aug 1850 in Alabama. She died on 15 Apr 1929 in San Antonio, Texas.

More About Lafayette Taylor Edwards:
Burial: 25 Jul 1916 in Mission Burial Park South, San Antonio,
Texas
Cause Of Death: Pellagra
Occupation: 1870 in Talbotton, Talbot County, Georgia; Working on his
mother's farm
Occupation: 1880 in Sumter County, Georgia; Farmer
Occupation: 1900 in San Antonio, Texas; Boarding House Keeper

5. **AMBROSE**[2] **EDWARDS** (William Newton[1]) was born on 16 Apr 1805 in Wilkes County, Georgia. He died on 06 Oct 1884 in Dale County, Alabama. He married Emeline James Gaulding, daughter of John Gaulding and Martha Gaulding in 1827 in South Carolina. She was born on 10 Feb 1810 in Virginia. She died on 01 Jan 1886 in Dale County, Alabama.

More About Ambrose Edwards:
Burial: Pleasant Hill Methodist Cemetery, Ozark,
Alabama
Living In: 1830 Talbot County, Georgia
Living In: 1840 Russell County, Alabama
Occupation: 1850 in Russell County, Alabama; Farmer
Occupation: 1860 in Dale County, Alabama; Farmer
Occupation: 1870 in Dale County, Alabama; Farmer
Occupation: 1880 in Dale County, Alabama; Farmer
Military Service: Matthews Company, Dale County Reserves, Dale County, Alabama C.S.A.
Property: 1850 in Russell County, Alabama; 150 Acres Improved and 252 Acres Unimproved
Property: 1860 in Dale County, Alabama; 260 Acres Improved and 260 Acres Unimproved
Property: 1870 in Dale County, Alabama; 1250 Acres Improved and 500 Acres Unimproved
Property: 1880 in Dale County, Alabama; 75 Acres Improved and 360 Acres Unimproved

Notes for Ambrose Edwards:
Originally buried in Pleasant Hill Cemetery near Westville, moved to new Pleasant Hill
Cemetery near Ozark in 1942 when Fort Rucker was established

Moved to Talbot County, Georgia in 1829.
Moved to Russell County, Alabama in 1839. This part of Russell County is now in Lee
County, Alabama
Moved to Dale County, Alabama near Westville in November 1854.

Obituary of Ambrose Edwards

Crittenden's Mill, Ala. December 7th 1884 (Published in the Southern Star, December 31,
1884)
Ambrose Edwards was born in Wilkes county Georgia, April 16th 1805 and died in Dale
county Alabama, October the 6th 1884, in triumphs of the Christian faith. He was happily married
to Emeline J. Gaulding October the 4th 1827 in Bibb county Georgia. In 1820 he moved to Talbot
county Georgia and in 1839 he settled in Russell county Alabama where he joined the Methodist
Episcopal Church and was Happily converted to God in which faith and communion he lived a
consistent and devoted member to the date of his death. He was the father of eleven children five
of whom have preceded him to the better land and the other six (all sons) are trying to follow in
the footsteps of their father: one a minister of the gospel: four are superintendents of Sabbath
schools and the other a church secretary.
No wife ever had a more devoted husband, no children a more affectionate father. His greatest
ambition in life was to do good and to see his children good and honorable. Of the seven boys he
raised to be men not a dram drinker nor a profane swearer was in the number. He was for many
years a practical steward of the church till the mantle fell on his oldest son. He was a man of great
will power but was always conservative in his intercourse with his fellow man. Few men were ever
more instrumental in settling difficulties between brethren and neighbors than he.

While he was deprived of an early education his practical good sence always gave him first rank in the county where he lived. The last thirty years of his life was spent in Dale county. The writer was with him day and night the greater portion of his last sickness: and such patience he hardly ever witnessed. The only thing that seemed to trouble his mind was leaving his aged and devoted companion who had shared his joys and sorrows through a married life of fifty-seven years. What a happy reunion it will be when the companion who still lingers on the shore of time only waiting for the summons, and the children all meet if faithful around the throne of God.

More About Emeline James Gaulding:
Burial: Pleasant Hill Methodist Cemetery, Ozark, Alabama

Notes for Emeline James Gaulding:
Originally buried in Pleasant Hill Cemetery near Westville, moved to new Pleasant Hill Cemetery near Ozark in 1942 when Fort Rucker was established.

Obituary of Emeline James Gaulding

Emeline J. Edwards, daughter of John Gaulding, was born in the state of Virginia in the month of February 1810. With her parents she removed to Hancock County Georgia in 1818. In that County she was converted at the age of eleven years and joined the Methodist E. Church, in which communion she lived sixty-four years without a stain upon her pure and spotless character. During the year 1827 she was married to Mr. Ambrose Edwards of Monroe County, Georgia. A few years after the happy event they removed to Alabama and settled in old Russell County. Although at the time of their marriage Mr. Edwards was not a member of any Church, not a professor in Jesus Christ, yet by her pure and sweet spirit he was so powerfully influenced in regard to salvation from sin and death as to become deeply concerned. At Salem, of old Russell County, 1839 he was converted and joined the Church of his Christian (.......?) In November 1854 they removed to Dale County and settled near Pleasant Hill Church and became members of that Church.

She was the mother of 11 children, 8 sons and 3 daughters, 5 of whom are dead and 6 living. All of those who lived to sufficient age joined the Church of their fond parents and are strong and devoted members of the Church. Such was the influence of the mother upon the whole family that they are perfectly united in affection, religion and cooperation. In this respect they constitute a model family. How ever distant from each other the children realize their unity in the mother. While breathing her last, a present was received, the gift of a son in Texas. As mother and grandmother she was an extraordinary woman. As wife she was all the Bible commands. As Church member and Christian she was perfect. To everybody she was tender, gentle and considerate. She always had a word of cheer and smile of appreciation for the toiling and struggling ones in righteousness. She heartily endorsed every enterprise of her Church and supported it's institution. Her Pastor always found her in sympathy with his efforts to build up the Church and save sinners. The writer has known her 30 years and knows no fault in her life. At 7 A. M. January 1, 1886 she ascended to glory. She died at the home of her son, C.A.B. Edwards, and was buried at Pleasant Hill on Saturday beside her husband, amid tears of sorrow and hope.

By Rev. Angus Dowling

Ambrose Edwards and Emeline James Gaulding had the following children:

    i. MARTHA LOUISE[3] EDWARDS was born on 20 Jul 1828 in Georgia. She died on 09 Aug 1881 in Alabama. She married Hope Hull Mizell, son of William Mizell and Mary Love on 07 Dec 1843 in Russell County, Alabama. He was born on 20 Sep 1820 in Baldwin County, Georgia. He died on 02 Mar 1887 in Haw Ridge, Alabama.

    More About Martha Louise Edwards:

b: 20 Jul 1848
Burial: Haw Ridge, Alabama

ii.   LEROY MARION EDWARDS was born on 29 Aug 1830 in Talbot County, Georgia. He died on 24 May 1898 in Brundidge, Alabama. He married Martha Mizell, daughter of William Mizell and Mary Love on 06 Nov 1849 in Russell County, Alabama. She was born on 04 Feb 1829 in Houston County, Georgia. She died on 30 Oct 1908 in Brundidge, Pike County, Alabama.

More About LeRoy Marion Edwards:
Burial: Pleasant Hill Methodist Cemetery, Ozark, Alabama
Occupation: 1850 in Russell County, Alabama; Farmer
Occupation: Bet. 1860-1880 in Dale County, Alabama; Farmer,
Occupation: 1866 Justice of the Peace, Dale County, Alabama. Commissioned July 6, 1866.
Occupation: 1891; Justice of the Peace, Dale County, Alabama. Appointed January 29, 1891, Commisioned February 13, 1891.
Occupation: Bet. 1893-1895 Served in Alabama State Legislature
Occupation: 1894 in Dale County, Alabama; County Superintendant of Education. Elected August 6, 1894 and commisioned September 19, 1894.
Military Service: Bet. 26 Aug 1862-1865; Co. E, 53rd Alabama Mounted Infantry, C.S.A.
Property: 1850 in Russell County, Alabama; 20 Acres Improved and 60 Acres Unimproved
Property: 1860 in Dale County, Alabama; 60 Acres Improved and 100 Acres Unimproved
Property: 1870 in Dale County, Alabama; 160 Acres Improved and 140 Acres Unimproved

Notes for LeRoy Marion Edwards:
    Promoted to the rank of the rank of Second Lieutenant in Company E, 53rd Alabama Mounted Infantry on November 15, 1863. (Alabama Partisan Rangers).

    Enlisted August 26, 1862 and served until the end of the War.

    Served in Alabama State Legislature 1893-1895 Served
as Justice of the Peace in Pike County, Alabama

    Died in the home of his daughter, Mary Love Edwards, while visiting her.
----

iii.   JOHN WILSON GAULDING EDWARDS was born on 10 Jan 1833 in Talbot County, Georgia. He died about 1858. He married Sarah Frances Sharp, daughter of Jehu Harrison Sharp and Tabitha Jane White on 04 Oct 1854 in Meriwether County, Georgia. She was born on 30 Oct 1836 in Georgia. She died on 09 Jul 1904 in Texas.

iv.   WILLIAM ARCHIBALD EDWARDS was born on 28 Feb 1835 in Talbot County, Georgia. He died on 12 Dec 1926 in Dallas, Texas. He married Eliza Jones White, daughter of Theophilus White and Mary H. Jett on 05 Jan 1858 in Russell County, Alabama. She was born on 08 Apr 1836 in Meriwether County, Georgia. She died on 06 Sep 1922 in Dallas, Texas.

More About William Archibald Edwards:
Burial: 14 Dec 1926 in Oak Cliff Cemetery, Dallas,
Texas
Occupation: 1861; Farmer
Occupation: 1870 in Autauga County, Alabama; Minister
Occupation: 1880 in Farmersville, Texas; School Teacher
Occupation: 1900 in Eagle Ford, Dallas County, Texas; Minister
Occupation: 1910 in Dallas, Dallas County, Texas; Retired
Occupation: 1920 in Dallas, Dallas County, Texas; Retired - Living with his
daughter Eliza and her husband George Cochran
Occupation: Methodist Minister
Military Service: Bet. 03 Jul 1861-13 Aug 1863; Company E, 15th
Alabama Infantry, C.S.A.

Notes for William Archibald Edwards:

Published in:
Southern Star, Jan. 5, 1916

Dallas, Tex., Nov. 11,
1915. Dear Ruf:
   I wrote you for a list of my dear old Co. E. 15th Alabama Regiment who are now
living, and as you were sick Bro. Charley Edwards sent me the following list vis.-
W.R. Painter, W.C. Mizell Ozark; J.R. Edwards, Mat Williams, Ariton; C. V.
Atkinson, Newton; Newt Curenton, Haw Ridge; Albert Austin, Daleville; W.D.
Byrd, B.W. Fleming, Enterprise; Dorse Fleming, Geneva; C.G. Dillard, Ozark
Route 1. To this I add the Texas list---Capt. Wm. A. Edwards, 4019 Bowser St.
Dallas Texas; A.N. Edwards, Gordon, Tex.;Y.M. Edwards, Alvin, Tex.; J.P. Martin,
Italy, Tex.; Ben Martin, Waxahachie, Tex.; Wm. Mobly Crandal Dallas County,
Tex. The above constitute the list of survivors as I have it. If you know of any
others please add them to this.
   The Company left home with 84 men enlisted all told 200. Returned home
after surrender 100. So you see 100 brave and as good men as Dale or any
other county ever raised sleep in some Northern or Southern cemetery or in
shallow crude graves on some battle field, or possibly some were buried
under the winter snow or to decay on some bloody hard fought battle ground and
their bones to bleach under a burning sun, and to their dust and memory we say
farewell dear comrades, and we hope some day to meet you beyond the flash
and roar of artillery and rattle of musketry.
   It will probably be some interest to the friends and survivors of Co. E. to read a
short write up of the Company which I hope you will have the Star to publish and send
a copy to all living members. I t will likely be the last message they will ever get from
me as I am now past eighty and they are not in their teens. I want each to take this as
a personal letter and I would be glad to have a letter from all of them.
   No better Co. of citizens soldiers ever left any community than left Westville
on the 18th day of July 1861, 54 years ago the past July. No more sumptuous
feast was ever spread for departing patriots than was spread under the shade
of the beautiful oaks that stood around old Darian Church. The
loving hands that prepared it have long since been wafted beyond the curse of war
and rage of battles by the angels of God. In all my life I have never seen deeper and
purer emotions or heard so tender farewells as followed that sumptuous feast.
Husbands and wives embraced in tender love and with many it was the last embrace--
-fathers kissed their only babes---mothers threw a mothers arm around her son and
with a mothers deep prayer sent her soldier boy to the conflict of battle and perils of
war. And some of the boys felt the tender touch of the bride-to-be as they clasped
hands that day. It thrilled their souls and nerved their arm for deeds of daring until they
either perished in the campaign or returned home under the furled

banner of the stars and bars. I have often been anxious to know if any of them that got back got left. "That day many parted, Where few shall meet."

That night we camped at Fraziers mill on Pea river and almost the entire company took a bath, and if there were either snakes, alligators or varmints for miles around they took to the hills and swamps never to return. Such a babel of voices and splashing of water I have never heard. The next night we camped in the open streets of Perote, and its bests families welcomed us with royal favors, and our third night out we stopped at Union Springs and spent the Sabbath there, which stay will always be kindly remembered by

Co.E. That was the day of the first Manassas battle and Bull Run episode. Many thought the war was ended and some kind hearted mothers hoped their boys might see Richmond before they were disbanded. Well the boys saw Richmond and beyond. How little we knew of war and the bitter cup before the south.

We next find ourselves organized as Co. E. in the 15th Alabama Regiment. Nothing of special interest to the Co. E until our regiment camped at Camp Toombs between Centerville and Manassas. There Dick Neil died. This is worthy of mentioning because he was the first member of Co. E that died and the first one that had died in a regimental camp. He was honored as but few soldiers are ever honored. The Regiment was drawn up to witness the solemn burial, and Co. E with reversed arms and muffled drum followed the corpse to

the road that leads from Centerville to Manassas; and there in plain coffin with a soldiers blanket for a winding sheet we buried him and a platoon of Co. E fired a soldier salute about the lonely grave, and there on the lonely spot unmarked by human hands and unknown to the busy world that passes that way to-day sleeps the dust of Corporal Neil without a stain on his name or character at home or in the army. It was the first crude shock that came to Co. E and it threw a gloom over the folks at home as nothing had done. All began to realize that war was on, and I remember at that camp Col. Canty told me it would be a terrible struggle. We spent the winter at Manassas and the only thing of special interest to Co. E was the task of getting boards for winter quarters, a task I never heard a single member complain

of.

I was sent with my Company across Bull Run to the east of Centerville in the hilly and wooded country that had been but little occupied by soldiers up to that time, to get boards to cover huts for winter quarters. And old federal sympathizer lived about half a mile from our camp and killed hogs one day, it would have been better had he killed all he had. I went up to his house and wanted to buy a hasslet. He asked 50 cents for it and at that time we thought ten or fifteen cents good pay. I went back where the boys were at work and related what had occurred and I saw one of them give a significant wink and asked "Do you love hasslet Captain and I told him yes." Well to make a long story short, next morning when I woke up there was a ham

of a 250 pound hog slipped under my tent and a large hasslet hanging in front and John Trawick, my cook, singing, whistling and frying liver and ham just as happy as he could get and you remember John could get very happy. I ate it and asked no questions for conscience sake, and as well as I remember it was the first and last stolen meat I ate during the war.

1862 was the fighting year of the war. Before the ground had thawed and the buds had burst into leaves we were taken from our pleasant quarters and transferred to the valley and received a formal introduction to Stonewall Jackson. There are two incidents in this campaign I wish to relate, not battles the historian does that, but unnoticed and unknown to the historian yet of interest to the Co. E. I allude to the death of Jno. Trawick and Lieut. Mills. John Trawick was killed almost under the guns of Harper Ferry, when we halted in our pursuit of Banks. We were resting on the turn-pike when a gun accidentally discharged and shattered poor Johns heel to pieces. He was carried to a Winchester Hospital, and in a few days I received notice he was dead.

I want to say this for John Trawick, I detailed him to cook for me, and he did more for my comfort than any one else has ever done. He carried my luggage on marches. (He was big and strong.) When the Regiment halted if it was mid-night. He spread my bedding and cooked my supper no matter how tired he was, and I have often wondered if Israel's chariot was sent down to take that rough, rugged yet noble son of nature to a bright and better world.

Lieut. Mills was killed at Cross Keys, when an unexpected retreat was ordered our regiment. He was a hightoned, brave Christian gentlemen confided in at home and honored and loved in the army. He was devoted to his mess and his mess to him quiet, intelligent, refined and dignified a high type of a Christian gentleman yet he always impressed me that a cloud was over his spirits an I have never thought he expected to survive the war, and I thought and still think that terrible specter of presentment was ever before his eyes.

At night after the terrible battle of Gains Mills at Richmond after night fall had covered the field of carnage and death which was strewed with dead and dying, I fell on Billy Robinson, a fine specimen of manhood, tall, angular swarthy, hair as black as a crow and fearless as a lion. He told me he was mortally wounded and could live but a little while. He asked me who held the field I told him we held it. Then he said I am willing to die. Tell father I died fighting for my home and country, that I died brave and I feel I am prepared for a better world. His father was a Methodist preacher.

Co. E did the fighting for Hood's division at Suffolk. It held the line against great odds early morning till night, did the picket duty till mid night and covered the retreat of the army twenty or twenty five to Black Water River. I doubt if any Company ever withstood so strong and persistent attack, more courageously and firmly than did Co. E. A whole brigade against one company for an entire day, but we had the position on them.

During the engagement I met Jess Flowers, hat off sleeves rolled up, and sweat rolling from his brow. He said Captain they have killed my mess mate Cameron, and I am ready to fight the whole Yankee army. I believe Jess would have tried it. Cameron was a good man and soldier and died with his face to the enemy. The only three men I detailed to cook for me were Trawick, Flowers and Charley Jones; the two first were killed and Charley Jones crippled for life.

While we were at Suffolk, the battle of the wilderness was fought and fighting Joe Hooper whipped. Thence we followed Lee to Gettysburg, which with the surrender of Fort Donaldson sealed the fate of the Confederacy. They first brought Grant, the man of destiny into the lime light, and second, settled the question of invasion, and so reduced Lee's army that it was only a question of time when it would succumb to superior force. But I wish to say a few things about that great and fatal battle. First the 15th,
Alabama went further in that battle than any other troop, second Co. E went as far as any part of the Regiment and staid as long. The men fired their guns until the barrel become so hot they could not hold and load them.

The death of private Holloway was to me the saddest feature of this sanguinary struggle. We were well protected behind a great rock about 4 feet high, the enemy equally protected behind a rock fence not more than 50 yards in front of us, and Captain Park reported a flanking division (Sickles) coming in our rear. Col. Oats ordered a charge and mounted the rock himself and discharged the contents of a six shooter in the face of the enemy. No one would follow but Holloway who mounted the rock, fell on his left knee, fixed his musket and a ball from the enemy crashed through his left temple and he fell dead at the feet of his gallant Colonel. How gallant! How useless! I saw the gallant deed and in the rage of battle and reign of death I thought what a sorrow it would carry to the bereaved wife and ten orphaned children far away in our beloved Alabama.

But our hearts were not always heavy and our heads bowed with grief. The soldier out of battle was ready for favor and the evening before the Gettysburg battle Co. E. was out on picket line.

Gen. Lee had ordered no private property disturbed and among the grove of large oaks in which [we] were camped a bunch of fine hogs had been browsing for acorns all day. Co. E's mouth had been watering all day for a taste of Yankee pork. Late that evening the Colonel told me there would be rations that evening and to let any one kill one of those hogs. I called the Co. together and told them to kill one of the biggest hogs and before I could stop then they had killed three and had a fourth so nearly dead I allowed them to finish it. But a very amazing thing occurred during the hog killing. I had two men in my Company, some of you may still remember them for no Company could well be without two such men. One was Sam Hog a great big over grown man, and Peters a small little fellow, and I looked out and saw Peters coming towards me closely pursued by Hog, nearly in touching distance and at every leap he would cry "help me Captain! Help me Captain." I called a halt-inquired the trouble, Hog said Peters hit him with a rock and nearly broke his leg, and Peters gasping for breath said "Captain you told us to kill the biggest hog we could find and he was the biggest one I saw. It was so ludicrous Hog burst into loud laughter and limping turned to his quarters. The truth was Peters had missed his mark.

One more incident that was very amusing to me, and the strange part isit never cease to be amusing to me. The parties to this incident were uncle Dave Snell and Latimer, both as true and worth men as ever girded their shoes with the accentments of war or shouldered a musket, both are now under the soil beyond the din of battle.

One morning at roll call Latimer came up with a broken arm and it was broken after the rest of the Company had gone to bed, Uncle Dave was to report the case and with the usual gravity of old men. He said he and Latimer went to the spring to get water to cook and coming up from the spring with a bucket of water his foot slipped, he fell and broke his arm. No one dared question Uncle Dave's word, but it seemed strange to me they should be out at midnight after water to cook, I said nothing knowing full well if it had any rich or racy features the boys could not keep it from me. So I pretty soon got a full statement of the case, and not very much like Uncle Dave's. They had gone to a nearby apple orchard and Latimer climbed a tree and sized a hornets' nest and in his hasty retreat a limb broke, he fell and broke his arm. A few days after on the march I asked the old soldier to tell me exactly how the accident occurred and with great precision he related the affair to where Latimer started up the hill with his camp kettle of water and said "Captain he got slickest fall I ever saw." Well says I, Uncle Dave were there any hornets about the spring. "Captain he said I'll tell you all about it. I told him no I knew it all. I never blamed him not Latimer only for not knowing the difference between an apple and a hornet nest. In fact I never blamed Adam so much for eating that red apple Eve gave him, I expect I would have done as he did. This occurred as well as I remember at Raccoon ford of the Rapidan.

In conclusion of this article to my old true and tried friends and comrades-friends and soldiers tried in the crucible of fire. There are a few things I reflect on with great pleasure.

1st, after the surrender Co. E returned from the scenes of battle and war, with true manhood and moral character and honest purpose entered honorable business and have been successful and useful citizens.

2nd, that my original mess eight of us are still living and constitute nearly half of the now living members of the Company.

3rd, and last and by far the most pleasing reflection is that I treated my Company as gentlemen, They were gentlemen at home and I could see no reason why they should not be treated as gentlemen in the army and I do not remember having punished one of my men, I consciously believed discipline could be maintained without it, and I do not believe the Confederacy ever produced a better Company on the march a more orderly one in camps, nor a braver one in battle, and soon the last of us will hear the tatoo for final sleep and rest, and the revilee. When the trumpet of God shall awake and the sleeping dust of earths millions, and may we answer the roll call on that side of the river that makes glad the city of God.

Wm. A. EDWARDS

First Lieutenant July 3, 1861; Captain March 6, 1862; Resigned September 2, 1863 and served as Chaplain for the duration of the War.

Enlisted on July 3, 1861 at Fort Mitchell, Alabama and served until resigning to become Chaplain on September 2, 1863.

Engagements: Winchester, Cross Keys, Cold Harbor, Fredericksburg, Suffolk, Hazel River, 2nd Manassas, Chantilly, Harpers Ferry, Sharpsburg, Shepardstown, Gettysburg, Battle Mount.

Pre War residence was Westville, Alabama.

June 3-August 1, 1863 -- The Gettysburg Campaign.
No. 444.--Report of Col. William C. Oates, Fifteenth Alabama Infantry.

AUGUST 8,
1863.

SIR: I have the honor to report, in obedience to orders from brigade headquarters, the participation of my regiment in the battle near Gettysburg on the 2d ultimo. My regiment occupied the center of the brigade when the line of battle was formed. During the advance, the two regiments on my right were moved by the left flank across my rear, which threw me on the extreme right of the whole line. I encountered the enemy's sharpshooters posted behind a stone fence, and sustained some loss thereby. It was here that Lieut. Col. Isaac B. Feagin, a most excellent and gallant officer, received a severe wound in the right knee, which caused him to lose his leg. Privates (A.) Kennedy, of Company B, and (William) Trimner, of Company G, were killed at this point, and Private (G. E.) Spencer, Company D, severely wounded. After crossing the fence, I received an order from Brigadier-General Law to left-wheel my regiment and move in the direction of the heights upon my left, which order I failed to obey, for the reason that when I received it I was rapidly advancing up the mountain, and in my front I discovered a heavy force of the enemy. Besides this, there was great difficulty in accomplishing the maneuver at that moment, as the regiment on my left (Forty-seventh Alabama) was crowding me on the left, and running into my regiment, which had already created considerable confusion. In the event that I had obeyed the order, I should have come in contact with the regiment on my left, and also have exposed my right flank to an enfilading fire from the enemy. I therefore continued to press forward, my right passing over the top of the mountain, on the right of the line. On reaching the foot of the mountain below, I found the enemy in heavy force, posted in rear of large rocks upon a slight elevation beyond a depression of some 300 yards in width between the base of the mountain and the open plain beyond. I engaged them, my right meeting the left of their line exactly. Here I lost several gallant officers and men. After firing two or three rounds, I discovered that the enemy were giving way in my front. I ordered a charge, and the enemy in my front fled, but that portion of his line confronting the two companies on my left held their ground, and continued a most galling fire upon my left. Just at this moment, I discovered the regiment on my left (Forty-seventh Alabama) retiring. I halted my regiment as its left reached a very large rock, and ordered a left-wheel of the regiment, which was executed in good order under fire, thus taking advantage of a ledge of rocks running off in a line perpendicular to the one I had just abandoned, and affording very good protection to my men. This position enabled me to keep up a constant flank and cross fire upon the enemy, which in less than five minutes caused him to change front. Receiving reinforcements, he charged me five times, and was as often repulsed with heavy loss. Finally, I discovered that the enemy had flanked me on the right, and two regiments were moving rapidly upon my rear and not 200 yards distant, when, to save my regiment from capture or destruction, I ordered a retreat. Having become exhausted from fatigue and the excessive heat of the day, I turned the command of the regiment over to Capt. B. A. Hill, and instructed him to take the men off the field, and reform the regiment and report to the brigade.

My loss was, as near as can now be ascertained, as follows, to wit: 17 killed upon the field, 54 wounded and brought off the field, and 90 missing, most of whom are either killed or wounded. Among the killed and wounded are 8 officers, most of whom were very gallant and efficient men.

Recapitulation.--Killed, 17; wounded, 54; missing, 90; total, 161.

I am, lieutenant, most respectfully, your obedient servant,

W. C. OATES,
Colonel, Commanding Fifteenth Alabama Regiment

Lieut. B.O. PETERSON,
Acting Assistant Adjutant-General

----

v.   MARY CLEMENTINE EDWARDS was born on 06 Dec 1836 in Talbot County, Georgia. She died on 27 Sep 1871 in Statesville, Alabama. She married Mordecai White, son of Theophilus White and Mary H. Jett on 17 Mar 1853. He was born on 02 Sep 1829 in Brunswick County, Georgia. He died on 06 Jan 1896 in Autauga County, Alabama.

More About Mary Clementine Edwards:
Burial: Love Family Cemetery, Mulberry, Autauga County, Alabama

Notes for Mary Clementine Edwards:
Died of burns received while protecting her children when a kerosene lamp exploded.
----

vi.   SARAH E. EDWARDS was born on 06 Aug 1838 in Talbot County, Georgia. She died in Jun 1849 in Alabama.

vii. AMBROSE NEWTON EDWARDS was born on 21 Oct 1840 in Russell County, Alabama. He died on 20 Jul 1933 in Strawn, Texas. He married Joanna Columbia Ardis, daughter of Isaac Ardis and Jane Elizabeth White on 05 Dec 1865 in Dale County, Alabama. She was born on 04 Feb 1847 in Salem, Alabama. She died on 08 Aug 1922 in Greenville, Texas.

More About Ambrose Newton Edwards:
Burial: 21 Jul 1933 in Forest Park Cemetery, Greenville, Texas- Moved later to Restland Cemetery, Dallas, Texas
Cause Of Death: Prostate Cancer
Occupation: 1860 in Dale County, Alabama; School Teacher
Occupation: 1870 in Sulphur Springs, Texas; Dry Goods Merchant
Occupation: 1880 in Hopkins County, Texas; County Clerk
Occupation: Bet. 27 Mar 1886-20 Oct 1891 ; Postmaster, Eliasville, Texas
Occupation: 1900 in Palo Pinto County, Texas; Lumber Dealer
Occupation: 1910 in Gordon, Palo Pinto County, Texas; Lumber Merchant
Occupation: 1920 in Palo Pinto County, Texas; Retired
Occupation: 1930 in Greenville, Texas; Retired - Living with his son, Ambrose Edwin Edwards
Military Service: Bet. 03 Jul 1861-11 Jun 1865 in C.S.A.; Company E, 15th Alabama Infantry

Notes for Ambrose Newton Edwards:
    Enlisted on July 3, 1861 in Westville, Alabama and served until July 2, 1863 when he was captured at Gettysburg, Pennsylvania and made a prisoner of war. Sent first to Fort McHenry, Maryland on July 5, 1863 and then to Fort Delaware, Delaware on July 6, 1863. Released from Fort Delaware on June 11, 1865.

    Engagements: Winchester, Cross Keys, Harpers Ferry, Sharpsburg, Fredericksburg, Suffolk, Malvern Hill, Cedar Mt. Hazel River, 2nd Manassas, Chantilly, Gettysburg.

    Wounded at Sharpsburg.and Fredericksburg.

    Promoted to Second Sergeant May 15, 1862.
    Promoted to First Sergeant July 25, 1862.
    Promoted to Second Lieutenant but was captured at Gettysburg, Pennsylvania before his commission arrived.

    Pre Civil War Residence was Westville, Alabama.

    Flag of the Army of Northern Virginia covered his casket during his first funeral and burial at Greeneville, Texas.

    Member of the first Board of Regents for the University of Texas 1881-1882

    Buried in Greenville, Texas in 1933 and then buried in Restland Cemetery, Dallas, Texas on February 9, 1955, grave marker set on August 31, 1955.

    Became a Mason at Brightstar Lodge number 221 in Sulphur Springs, Texas on November 5, 1868.

    Death certificate gives October 18, 1840 as date of birth.

                    Dictated to Emma Irene Garland (Edwards) in 1930

I well remember the day when my company assembled at old Darian Church in Dale County, Alabama, where we bade good bye to our loved ones and took up our march to the battle front in answer to our country's call.

I remember the first night we camped on the banks of Pea River and bathed in its waters and spent this our first night in joyous hilarity. I remember after three days march we reached old Fort Mitchell near Columbus Georgia, where we were organized into the 15th Alabama Infantry, my company being known as co. E. Then after a few weeks of company and regimental drill we had orders to go to Virginia, and this was for me a matter of exquisite thrill and interest which cannot be well depicted here.

When we reached Richmond we were quartered at Old Chimborozo where we remained about three weeks and thence to Manassas. Shortly after the noted first battle of the war, as there was no more fighting in this section, we went into winter quarters there. Up to this time we had not had to suffer any great hardships, but had many interesting experiences.

In the beginning of 1862, the second year of the war, greater activities in war matters became more tense. McClelland was assembling a great army in the Yorktown peninsula with the purpose of marching on to Richmond and General Johnson was ordered to fall back from Manassas to meet this move of the enemy. But Ewell's division, to which I belonged, was ordered to join Stonewall Jackson in the valley. Then my regiment was in the noted Valley campaign in which Jackson defeated three armies and then it was at Cross Keys we received our baptism of battle. From here the scene changed and the Seven days battle around Richmond was fought in which my regiment took an active part and lost quite a number of noble men.

I was sick and in the hospital at Charlottesville at that time. After McClelland's defeat General Lee moved his army North. On the first invasion. we crossed the Potomac at Leesburg, wading it of course as there were no bridges. My division was ordered to go around and cross back above Harper's Ferry where General Wool was stationed with seven thousand men. We had him completely surrounded and he surrendered. In this surrender we secured arms, commissary, and quarter master supplies in great abundance.

Immediately after the surrender we were ordered back across the Potomac to be in the battle of Sharpsburg - called Antietam by the North Historians - this was one of the hardest battles of the war, and was known as a draw. Lee withdrew to the Virginia side and there ended that year's campaign in Virginia.

To avoid being tedious, I will omit many important military operations including the battle of Fredericksburg in which i took a part and will speak of the Pennsylvania invasion and the battle of Gettysburg. I was in this battle and on the second day of July 1863, with thirteen other men of my company was captured and carried to Fort Delaware where we were kept as prisoners until the war closed.

I could make an interesting chapter about our prison, but only say we managed to keep up spirit and hope amid its trials and troubles until the day came for our release nearly two months after the surrender.

I reached home on the 5th of June 1865, to find our beloved Southland wrecked and ruined by war's devastation.

Then it was with unflinching courage we took up the task of reconstructing the ruin and building our new South upon it. While I cannot elaborate on this work, for it would require many words, yet I cannot omit saying that the work was done in a way that solicited the admiration of all people. Our noble women were our staunch co-laborers in every sense, and deserve a monument for their wonderful work.

On the 5th of December 1865 it was my good fortune to lead to the marriage alter one of the best of the noble daughters of the South, to walk with me and share with me, every joy and every sorrow that awaited us on lifes pilgrimage. We came to Texas in 1866 where eight sons came to bless our union, all noble men and all living useful lives in Texas except one. Eight years ago my precious one left me to go and wear her crown.

Now in my 90th year I can truly say that much love and kindness have been meted out to me, but must say that the best friends we old veterans have are the noble Daughters of the Confederacy, and may god bless them in my closing word.

A. N. Edwards
Co. E. 15th Alabama Inf.

----

viii.   YOUNG MANSFIELD EDWARDS was born in May 1843 in Russell County, Alabama. He died on 22 Feb 1923 in Sulphur Springs, Hopkins County, Texas. He married Martha E. Ardis, daughter of Archibald McCoy Ardis and Joanna Leticia White on 05 Dec 1865 in Dale County, Alabama. She was born on 25 Feb 1843 in Russell County, Alabama. She died on 27 Jan 1903 in Brazoria County, Texas.

More About Young Mansfield Edwards:
Burial: 22 Feb 1923 in City Cemetery, Sulphur Springs, Texas, 1C, Lot 40
Cause Of Death: Kidney Failure (Brights Disease)
Occupation: 1870 in Bright Star, Texas (Present Day Sulphur Springs, Texas); School Teacher
Occupation: 1880 in Sulphur Springs, Texas; Merchant
Occupation: 1900 in Brazoria County, Texas; Farmer
Occupation: 1910 in Brazoria County, Texas; Farm Laborer
Occupation: 1920 in Sulphur Springs, Texas; None, living with his brother in law, Henry Love Ardis.
Military Service: Bet. 03 Jul 1861-09 Apr 1865 ; Company E. 15th Alabama Infantry, C.S.A.

Notes for Young Mansfield Edwards:
    Captured near Knoxville, Tennessee November 29, 1863 and imprisoned at Fort Delaware. Exchanged on October 10, 1864 and rejoined Company E, 15th Alabama Infantry, serving until the surrender of the Army of Northern Virginia at Appomattox Court House.

    Enlisted in Company E, 15th Alabama Infantry at Fort Mitchell, Alabama on July 3, 1861.

    Engagements: Winchester, Cross Keys, Cold Harbor, Malvern Hill, Cedar Mountain, Hazel River, Second Manasses Junction, Chantilly, Harper's Ferry, Sharpsburg, Fredericksburg, Suffolk, Battle Mount, Chicamauga, Raccoon Mountain, Lookout Valley, Camel Station, Knoxville.

    Wounded at Sharpsburg.and Fredericksburg.

    Pre War residence was Westville, Alabama

    Had no children.

ix.   JAMES CARTER EDWARDS was born on 20 Sep 1844 in Russell County, Alabama. He died about 1854.

x.   CHARLES ANDERSON BROWN EDWARDS was born on 25 Oct 1846 in Russell County, Alabama. He died on 23 Dec 1937 in Dothan, Alabama. He married Martha Caroline Crittenden, daughter of Cincinnatus Decatur Crittenden and Emeline Amanda Mahone on 01 Sep 1867 in Ozark, Alabama. She was born on 09 Feb 1851 in Schley County, Georgia. She died on 04 Apr 1929 in Ozark, Alabama.

More About Charles Anderson Brown Edwards:
Burial: 24 Dec 1937 in Morning View Cemetery, Ozark, Alabama
Occupation: 1870 in Dale County, Alabama; Farmer
Occupation: 1880 in Daleville, Dale County, Alabama; Farmer
Occupation: 1900 in Daleville, Dale County, Alabama; Farmer
Occupation: 1910 in Ozark, Alabama; Farmer
Occupation: Bet. 16 Jan 1911-16 Jan 1917 in Dale County, Alabama; Probate Judge
Occupation: 1920 in Ozark, Alabama; Retired
Occupation: 1930 in Ozark, Alabama; Retired
Military Service: Bef. Feb 1864; Company A., Goldson's Alabama Battalion
Military Service: Bet. Feb 1864-05 May 1865; Company A, Brown's Independent Cavalry, Davidson's Battalion, Alabama Cavalry
Property: 1870 in Dale County, Alabama; 100 Acres Improved and 230 Acres Unimproved

Notes for Charles Anderson Brown Edwards:
Served two terms in the Alabama state legislature from Dale County; 1887-1889 and 1890-1891.

Paroled May 5, 1865 at Eufaula, Alabama.
----

xi.   WALTER STARR EDWARDS was born on 09 Sep 1850 in Russell County, Alabama. He died on 21 Sep 1927 in Geneva, Geneva County, Alabama. He married Sarah Frances Brown on 08 Jan 1871. She was born on 10 May 1853 in Georgia. She died on 30 May 1920 in Enterprise, Alabama.

More About Walter Starr Edwards:
Burial: Enterprise City Cemetery, Enterprise, Alabama
Occupation: 1870 in Westville, Dale County, Alabama; School Teacher
Occupation: 1880 in Westville, Dale County, Alabama; Farmer
Occupation: 1892; Superintendent of Education, Coffee County, Alabama. Elected August 1, 1892 and commissioned August 25, 1892.
Occupation: 1894 in Coffee County, Alabama; County Superintendant of Education. Elected August 6, 1894 and commisioned September 25, 1894.
Occupation: 1900 in Enterprise, Alabama; Timber Agent
Occupation: 1903; Notary Public, Enterprise, Alabama. Appointed February 28, 1903 and commissioned March 6, 1903.
Occupation: 1910 in Enterprise, Alabama; Life Insurance Agent
Occupation: 1920 in Enterprise, Alabama; City Clerk
Property: 1880 in Dale County, Alabama; 65 Acres Improved and 70 Acres Unimproved

Notes for Walter Starr Edwards:
Death record gives Geneva, Geneva County, Alabama as place of death.

6.   **MICHAEL**^{2} **EDWARDS** (William Newton^1) was born on 24 Mar 1810 in Georgia. He died in 1854 in Russell County, Alabama. He married Matilda Adams on 01 Oct 1837 in Talbot County, Georgia. She was born on 20 Dec 1821 in North Carolina. She died on 03 Mar 1901 in Alabama.

More About Michael Edwards:
Occupation: 1840 in Talbot County, Georgia; Farmer
Occupation: 1850; Farmer, Russell County, Alabama
Property: 1850 in Russell County, Alabama; 30 Acres Improved and 60 Acres Unimproved

More About Matilda Adams:
Burial: Leon Cemetery, Leon, Crenshaw County, Alabama
Living In: 1900 Living with John A. Hollis and his family in Leon, Crenshaw County, Alabama.

More About Michael Edwards and Matilda Adams:
Marriage Fact: Married by Robert Fleming (MG)

Michael Edwards and Matilda Adams had the following children:

   i.   ELMEDA^3 EDWARDS was born about 1839 in Alabama.

   ii.   MARY EDWARDS was born about 1841 in Alabama.

   iii. ELLEN EDWARDS was born about 1843 in Alabama.

         More About Ellen Edwards:
         Living In: 1870 Living with her mother and step father in Tanyard, Pike County, Alabama.

   iv.   WILLIAM EDWARDS was born about 1845 in Alabama.

   v.   GEORGIA EDWARDS was born about 1847 in Alabama.

   vi.   PERMILIA EDWARDS was born about 1849 in Alabama.

7.   **MARY**^{2} **EDWARDS** (William Newton^1) was born on 16 May 1815 in Georgia. She died before 18 Feb 1875 in Alabama. She married **WILLIAM ROBINSON**. He was born about 1815. He died before 25 Jan 1850. She married (2) **WILLIAM C. CLEGHORN** on 08 Sep 1852 in Russell County, Alabama. He was born on 22 Apr 1832 in Hall County, Georgia. He died on 19 Jul 1910 in Macon County, Alabama.

More About Mary Edwards:
Occupation: 1850 in Russell County, Alabama; Farmer

William Robinson and Mary Edwards had the following children:

   i.   WILLIAM C.^{3} ROBINSON was born in Nov 1839 in Alabama. He died in Alabama.

         More About William C. Robinson:
         Living In: 1850 Living with his uncle, Wilson B. Edwards, in Russell County, Alabama.

ii.   JAMES ROBINSON was born about 1841 in Alabama.

iii.   MISSOURI ELIZABETH ROBINSON was born about 1842 in Alabama. She died between 30 Jul 1870-09 Jul 1880 in Alabama. She married James L. Childers on 18 Nov 1860 in Russell County, Alabama. He was born about 1826 in Georgia.

iv.   MILES WILBURN ROBINSON was born on 13 Oct 1843 in Georgia. He died on 29 Dec 1923 in Columbus, Georgia. He married (1) ELIZABETH MCBRYDE, daughter of Joseph A McBryde and Amanda White on 12 Jul 1864 in Russell County, Alabama. She was born on 09 Mar 1848 in Georgia. She died in May 1883 in Salem, Alabama. He married (2) FRANCES CORNELIA BISHOP, daughter of Joseph Westley Bishop and Elizabeth Jane Edwards on 15 Aug 1883 in Columbus, Georgia. She was born on 03 Dec 1859 in Reeltown, Alabama. She died on 07 Nov 1945 in Phenix City, Russell County, Alabama.

More About Miles Wilburn Robinson:
Burial: 30 Dec 1923 in Pine Grove Cemetery, Phenix City, Russell County, Alabama
Occupation: 1870 in Auburn, Lee County, Alabama; Farmer
Occupation: 1880 in Brownville, Lee County, Alabama; Works in Cotton Mill
Occupation: 1900 in Opelika, Lee County, Alabama; Farmer
Occupation: 1910 in Salem, Lee County, Alabama; Retired
Occupation: 1920 in Columbus, Muscogee County, Georgia; Retired

Notes for Miles Wilburn Robinson:
Death certificate states Miles was born in Georgia but his family was living in Russell County, Alabama at the time of his birth.

v.   MARY JANE ROBINSON was born about 1849 in Alabama.

More About William C. Cleghorn:
Burial: Pleasant Springs Baptist Church Cemetery, Franklin, Macon County, Alabama
Occupation: 1860 in Russell County, Alabama; Farmer
Occupation: 1880 in Tuskegee, Macon County, Alabama; Farmer
Occupation: 1900 in Franklin, Macon County, Alabama; Farmer
Occupation: 1910 in Macon County, Alabama; Farmer
Military Service: Bet. 25 Jul 1863-1865 in Opelika, Alabama; Enlisted in Company H, 61st Alabama Infantry, C.S.A.
More About William C. Cleghorn and Mary Edwards:
Marriage Fact: Married by John Bevin J.P.

William C. Cleghorn and Mary Edwards had the following children:

i.   W. A.[3] CLEGHORN was born about 1852.

ii.   ELLEN O. CLEGHORN was born about 1855.

iii.   JOHN W. CLEGHORN was born about 1858. He married Victoria Hearn on 11 May 1879 in Macon County, Alabama.

iv.   A.T. CLEGHORN was born about 1859.

8.   ELIZABETH[2] EDWARDS (William Newton[1]) was born about 1818 in Georgia. She died after 03 Jun 1880. She married (1) **WILLIAM TROTTER**, son of William Trotter and (unknown) on 28 Dec 1843 in Talbot County, Georgia. He died in 1848. She married (2) **FELSTON PARKER** on 19 Dec 1849 in Russell County, Alabama. He was born on 12 Dec 1815 in North Carolina. He died before 09 Aug 1870.

More About Elizabeth
Edwards:
Living In: 1850 Russell County, Alabama with her second husband, Thelston Parker
Living In: 1860 Russell County, Alabama
Living In: 1870 Opelika, Lee County, Alabama
Living In: 1880 Pierce Chapel, Lee County, Alabama

Notes for William Trotter:
William Trotter died young and William's father was made guardian of his children.

More About William Trotter and Elizabeth Edwards:
Marriage License: 28 Dec 1843 in Talbot County, Georgia
Marriage Fact: Married by Charles A. Brown (M.G.)

William Trotter and Elizabeth Edwards had the following children:

    i.   MARY ANN[3] TROTTER was born about 1844 in Alabama. She married James M. Finch on 28 Sep 1858 in Russell County, Alabama.

    ii.   WHITFIELD TROTTER was born about 1846 in Alabama.

    iii.   NATHAN TROTTER was born about 1848 in Alabama.

More About Felston Parker:
Occupation: 1850 in Russell County, Alabama; Farmer
Occupation: 1860 in Russell County, Alabama; Farmer

More About Felston Parker and Elizabeth Edwards:
Marriage Contract: 18 Dec 1849 in Russell County, Alabama

Felston Parker and Elizabeth Edwards had the following children:

    i.   MARTHA[3] PARKER was born in Sep 1850 in Alabama. She married (UNKNOWN) BELVIN.

        More About Martha Parker:
        Living In: 1900 Living as a widow with her brother, George Parker, and his family in Pierce Chapel, Lee County, Alabama
        Living In: 1910 Living as a widow with her brother, George Parker, and his family in Grahams Store, Lee County, Alabama

    ii.   CAMILLA PARKER was born in Jan 1852 in Alabama. She married FRANCIS DEVLIN. He was born about 1855 in Massachusetts.

        More About Camilla Parker:
        Living In: 1900 Living as a widow in Pierce Chapel, Lee County, Alabama with her brother, George Parker, and his family.

Living In: 1930 Living as a widow with her brother, George Parker, and his family in Lee County, Alabama

iii.   FELSTON A. PARKER was born in 1854 in Alabama. He married Mary E. Holloway on 01 Apr 1880 in Lee County, Alabama.

iv.   WILSON M. PARKER was born in 1856 in Lee County, Alabama. He died on 15 Oct 1926 in LaGrange, Troup County, Georgia.

v.   JOHN A. W. PARKER was born on 15 Oct 1857 in Lee County, Alabama. He died on 21 Apr 1919 in Lee County, Alabama. He married Sarah (unknown) about 1880. She was born in Nov 1858 in Lee County, Alabama.

More About John A. W. Parker:
Living In: 1880 John and Sarah are living with John's mother in Pierce Chapel, Lee County, Alabama
Occupation: 1880 in Pierce Chapel, Lee County, Alabama; Saw Mill Worker
Occupation: 1900 in Pierce Chapel, Lee County, Alabama; Farmer
Occupation: 1910 in Grahams Store, Lee County, Alabama; Farmer

Notes for John A. W. Parker:
1900 U.S. census gives month and year of birth as October 1856.

vi.   JAMES MONROE PARKER was born on 16 Mar 1860 in Lee County, Alabama. He died on 06 May 1932 in Blontons, Lee County, Alabama. He married Aurilla E. Story about 1881 in Lee County, Alabama. She was born in Jul 1866 in Alabama.

More About James Monroe Parker:
Occupation: 1880 in Pierce Chapel, Lee County, Alabama; Farmer
Occupation: 1900 in Pierce Chapel, Lee County, Alabama; Farmer
Occupation: 1910 in Grahams Store, Lee County, Alabama; Farm Manager
Occupation: 1920 in Grahams Store, Lee County, Alabama; Farmer
Occupation: 1930 in Lee County, Alabama; Farmer

vii.   GEORGE HENRY L. PARKER was born on 17 Apr 1862 in Lee County, Alabama. He died on 30 Dec 1935 in Opelika, Lee County, Alabama. He married Laura E. Story, daughter of Daniel Brooks Story and Elizabeth R. Jones on 03 Nov 1889 in Lee County, Alabama. She was born on 26 Feb 1874 in Opelika, Lee County, Alabama. She died in 1937 in Lee County, Alabama.

More About George Henry L. Parker:
Burial: 31 Dec 1935 in Pierce Chapel Cemetery, Pierce Chapel, Alabama
Living In: 1935 Opelika, Alabama
Occupation: 1900 in Pierce Chapel, Lee County, Alabama; Farmer
Occupation: 1910 in Grahams Store, Lee County, Alabama; General Manager on Farm
Occupation: 1920 in Grahams Store, Lee County, Alabama; Farmer
Occupation: 1930 in Lee County, Alabama; Farmer

9.   SPENCER[2] EDWARDS (William Newton[1]) was born on 03 Apr 1817 in Georgia. He died on 02 Nov 1897 in Taylor County, Georgia. He married Mary Ann Willis, daughter of John E. Willis and Susanna H. Biggs on 25 Apr 1836 in Talbot County, Georgia. She was born about 1821 in

Georgia. She died before 1880.

More About Spencer Edwards:
Burial: Butler City Cemetery, Butler, Taylor County,
Georgia
Living In: 1866 Dale County, Alabama
Living In: 1880 Living with his son James R. Edwards, and his family in Westville, Dale county,
Alabama
Occupation: 1850 in Talbot County, Georgia; Farmer
Occupation: 1860 in Talbot County, Georgia; Farmer
Occupation: 1870 in Dale County, Alabama; Farmer
Occupation: 1883 in Haw Ridge, Alabama; Constable - Appointed and commissioned March
7, 1883.
Occupation: 1888 in Precinct 13, Coffee County, Alabama; Justice of the Peace - Elected
August 6, 1888.
Military Service: Indian War of 1836
Property: 1850 in Talbot County, Georgia; 35 Acres Improved and 15 Acres
Unimproved
Property: 1852 in Talbot County, Georgia; 150 Acres
Property: 1856 in Talbot County, Georgia; 95 Acres
Property: 1860 in Talbot County, Georgia; 35 Acres Improved and 15 Axcres Unimproved
Property: 1870 in Dale County, Alabama; 200 Acres Improved and 200 Acres Unimproved

Notes for Spencer Edwards:
Died while visiting A. J. Fountain in Taylor County, Georgia.

More About Spencer Edwards and Mary Ann Willis:
Marriage Fact: Married by G. B. Clay (J.P.)

Spencer Edwards and Mary Ann Willis had the following children:

    i.   JAMES RUSSELL[3] EDWARDS was born on 29 May 1840 in Russell County, Alabama. He died on 30 Jun 1926 in Lufkin, Angelina County, Texas. He married (1) SARAH ELIZABETH WHITE on 12 Jun 1866 in Alabama. She was born on 20 Feb 1840 in Alabama. She died on 06 Jul 1903 in Alabama. He married (2) MARY LOU SMITH, daughter of James Smith and Jane Trawick in Nov 1912 in Alabama. She was born on 05 Nov 1884 in Dale County, Alabama. She died on 21 Mar 1949 in Lufkin, Angelina County, Texas.

        More About James Russell Edwards:
        Burial: 01 Jul 1926 in Gann Cemetery, Lufkin, Angelina County,
        Texas
        Occupation: 1870 in Dale County, Alabama; Farmer
        Occupation: 1880 in Westville, Dale County, Alabama; Farmer
        Occupation: 1900 in Rocky Head, Dale County, Alabama; Farmer
        Occupation: 1910 in Rocky Head, Dale County, Alabama; Farmer
        Occupation: 1920 in Angelina County, Texas; Farmer
        Military Service: Bet. 03 Jul 1861-09 Apr 1865; Company E, 15th Alabama
        Infantry, C.S.A.
        Property: 1870 in Dale County, Alabama; 75 Acres Improved and 25
        Acres Unimproved

Notes for James Russell Edwards:

Enlisted in Company E, 15th Alabama Infantry, Fort Mitchell, Alabama on July 3, 1861 and served until the Army of Northern Virginia surrendered at Appomattox, Virginia on April 9, 1865. As the last remaining officer in the Company, James Russell Edwards surrendered Company E.

Promoted to 5th Sergeant on December 15, 1863.

Promoted to 2nd Segeant on June 15, 1864.

Elected second Lieutenant November 1, 1864.

Wounded at the Battle of the Wilderness May 3, 1864.

Engagements: Winchester, Cross Keys, Cold Harbor, Malvern Hill, Cedar Mountain, Hazel River, Second Manasses Junction, Chantilly, Harper's Ferry, Sharpsburg, Shepards Town, Fredericksburg, Suffolk, Gettysburg, Battle Mount, Chicamauga, Camel Station, Knoxville, Dandridge, Wilderness, Spotsylvania, 2nd Cold Harbor, Chester Station, Deepbottom, Fussell Mill, Fort Gilmer, Fort Hatison, Darbeytown, Darbeytown East Road, Williamsburg Road, Appomattox.

Pre War residence was Westville, Alabama

----

ii.   GREEN WILSON EDWARDS was born about 1844 in Georgia. He died in Dec 1869 in Dale County, Alabama. He married HARRIETT ELLEN BELCHER. She was born on 26 Jan 1847 in Florida. She died on 17 Nov 1909 in Enterprise, Alabama.

More About Green Wilson Edwards: Cause
Of Death: Hemorrhage From Cut

iii.   MARY EDWARDS was born about 1849 in Georgia.

iv.   NANCY EDWARDS was born about 1852 in Talbot County, Georgia.

v.   GEORGIA REBECCA EDWARDS was born on 14 May 1854 in Talbot County, Georgia. She died on 03 Apr 1941 in Daleville, Dale County, Alabama. She married JOHN GEORGE COTTEN. He was born on 18 Dec 1852 in Georgia. He died on 14 Jan 1926 in Enterprise, Coffee County, Alabama.

More About Georgia Rebecca Edwards:
b: 14 May 1854
Burial: Union Cemetery, Ozark, Dale County, Alabama
Living In: 1930 Living with her daughter, Marie, and her family in Daleville, Dale County, Alabama.
Living In: 1940 Living with her daughter, Marie, and her family in Clayhatchee, Dale County, Alabama.

vi.   ROBERT CHARLES EDWARDS was born on 11 May 1857 in Talbot County, Georgia. He died on 08 Dec 1931 in Enterprise, Alabama. He married Francesca La Coates about 1873. She was born in Aug 1860 in Texas. She died before Apr 1910.

More About Robert Charles Edwards: Burial:
09 Dec 1931 in Enterprise, Alabama
Living In: 1930   Enterprise, Alabama with his daughter Arie Anna and her husband.
Occupation: 1880 in Westville, Dale County, Alabama; Farmer
Occupation: 1900 in Haw Ridge, Coffee County, Alabama; Farmer
Occupation: 1910 in Enterprise, Alabama; Cross Tie Contractor
Occupation: 1930 in Enterprise, Alabama; Foreman at Peanut Mill

vii.   FRANCES V. EDWARDS was born about 1861 in Alabama.

Notes for Frances V. Edwards:
Living with James Russell Edwards and family in Westville, Alabama in June 1880.
----

10.   **WILSON B.**[2] **EDWARDS** (William Newton[1]) was born on 27 Jun 1821 in Georgia. He died on 16 Sep 1863 in Russell County, Alabama. He married Eleanor Aurora Trotter, daughter of William Trotter and (unknown) on 10 Aug 1843. She was born on 11 Apr 1823 in Russell County, Alabama. She died on 27 Oct 1873.

More About Wilson B. Edwards:
Occupation: 1850 in Russell County, Alabama; Farmer
Occupation: 1860 in Russell County, Alabama; Farmer
Property: 1850 in Russell County, Alabama; 30 Acres Improved and 30 Acres Unimproved
Property: 1860 in Russell County, Alabama; 175 Acres Improved and 115 Acres Unimproved

Notes for Wilson B. Edwards:
Died in the Civil War.

Estate was probated in Russell County, Alabama. Probate documents indicated his death was between August 1, 1863 and December 14, 1863.

Wilson B. Edwards and Eleanor Aurora Trotter had the following children:

i.   MARTHA ANN[3] EDWARDS was born on 02 Mar 1845 in Russell County, Alabama. She died on 15 Feb 1920 in Hopkins County, Texas. She married (1) SAMUEL B. PIPER on 17 Oct 1867 in Lee County, Alabama. He was born on 16 Aug 1831 in Georgia. He died on 28 Jan 1886 in Texas. She married (2) JAMES M. MORGAN, son of W. H. Morgan and Susan Cook on 27 Feb 1887 in Hopkins County, Texas. He was born on 08 Jul 1845 in Alabama. He died on 01 Mar 1925 in Sulphur Springs, Hopkins County, Texas.

More About Martha Ann Edwards:
Burial: Gafford Chapel Cemetery, Hopkins County, Texas

Notes for Martha Ann Edwards:
(Obituary - Mrs. J. M. Morgan, died Monday night at her home in the

western part of Sulphur Springs from pneumonia. She is survived by
her husband and several brothers and sisters in the county. She was
the second wife of J. M. Morgan and was an Edwards before her marriage.
The remains were buried at Gaffords Chapel Tuesday afternoon.
(Hopkins County Echo., Fri. Feb. 20, 1920)

----

ii. SPENCER W. EDWARDS was born in 1847 in Russell County, Alabama. He died
on 04 Apr 1865 in Macon, Georgia.

More About Spencer W. Edwards:
Cause Of Death: Rubella
Military Service: Company C, 14th Alabama Infantry, C.S.A.

Notes for Spencer W. Edwards:
Admitted to Milledgeville Military Hospital on March 16, 1865.
Transferred to Ocmulgee Military Hospital, Macon, Georgia, on March 25,
1865. Died of Rubella on April 4, 1865.

iii. MARY FRANCES EDWARDS was born about 1848 in Alabama.

iv. NANCY ELIZABETH EDWARDS was born in 1849 in Russell County, Alabama.

v. WILLIAM AMBROSE EDWARDS was born on 19 Aug 1851 in Alabama. He died on 13
Feb 1930 in Sulphur Springs, Hopkins County, Texas. He married Mary
Elizabeth Baylus in 1878 in Texas. She was born in Oct 1858 in Texas. She
died on 21 Dec 1936 in Hopkins County, Texas.

More About William Ambrose Edwards:
Burial: 14 Feb 1930 in Gafford Chapel Cemetery, Hopkins County,
Texas
Occupation: 1900; Farmer in Hopkins County, Texas

vi. WILSON WHITFIELD EDWARDS was born about 1856 in Alabama.

More About Wilson Whitfield Edwards:
Living In: 1880 Household of Samuel B. Piper in Hopkins County, Texas

vii. BISHOP ASBERRY EDWARDS was born about 1858 in Alabama.

More About Bishop Asberry Edwards:
Living In: 1880 Household of Samuel B. Piper in Hopkins County. Texas
Occupation: 1880; Farmer in Hopkins County, Texas

viii. ROBERT NEAL EDWARDS was born on 01 Jul 1860 in Opelika, Alabama. He died on
04 Oct 1931 in White Deer, Texas. He married XUMA VIRGINIA DENNIS. She was
born on 14 Jan 1870 in Gilmore, Texas. She died on 22 Oct 1956 in Amarillo,
Texas.

More About Robert Neal Edwards:
Burial: 05 Oct 1931 in White Deer Cemetery, White Deer, Carson County, Texas

Cause Of Death: Heart Failure
Living In: 1880 Household of Samuel B. Piper in Hopkins County, Texas
Occupation: Wheat Farmer

ix.   JAMES JOSEPH BONAPART EDWARDS was born about Jul 1863 in Russell County, Alabama. He died on 17 Mar 1943 in Tatum, Lea County, New Mexico. He married ESTA ELLEN BRAZELL. She was born in 1870 in Texas. She died in 1959 in New Mexico.

More About James Joseph Bonapart Edwards:
Burial: Tatum Cemetery, Tatum, Lea County, New Mexico
Living In: 1880 Household of Samuel B. Piper in Hopkins County, Texas

Notes for James Joseph Bonapart Edwards:
1900 U.S. census has month and year of birth as July 1863.
----

www.ingramcontent.com/pod-product-compliance
Lightning Source LLC
Chambersburg PA
CBHW080819280726
48660CB00018B/3535